Dip, Tip, Pat

by Joanna Lake

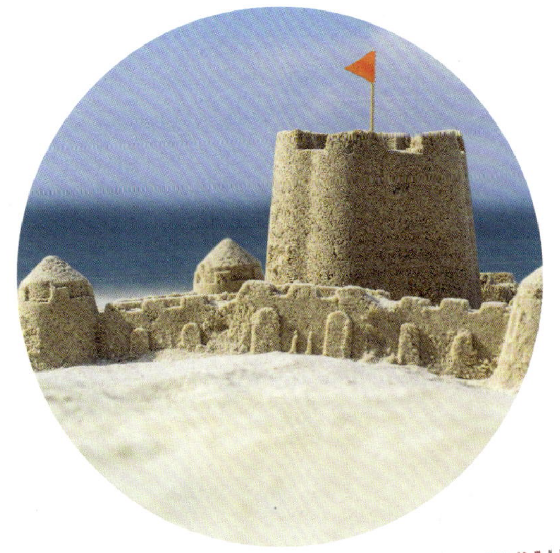

OXFORD
UNIVERSITY PRESS

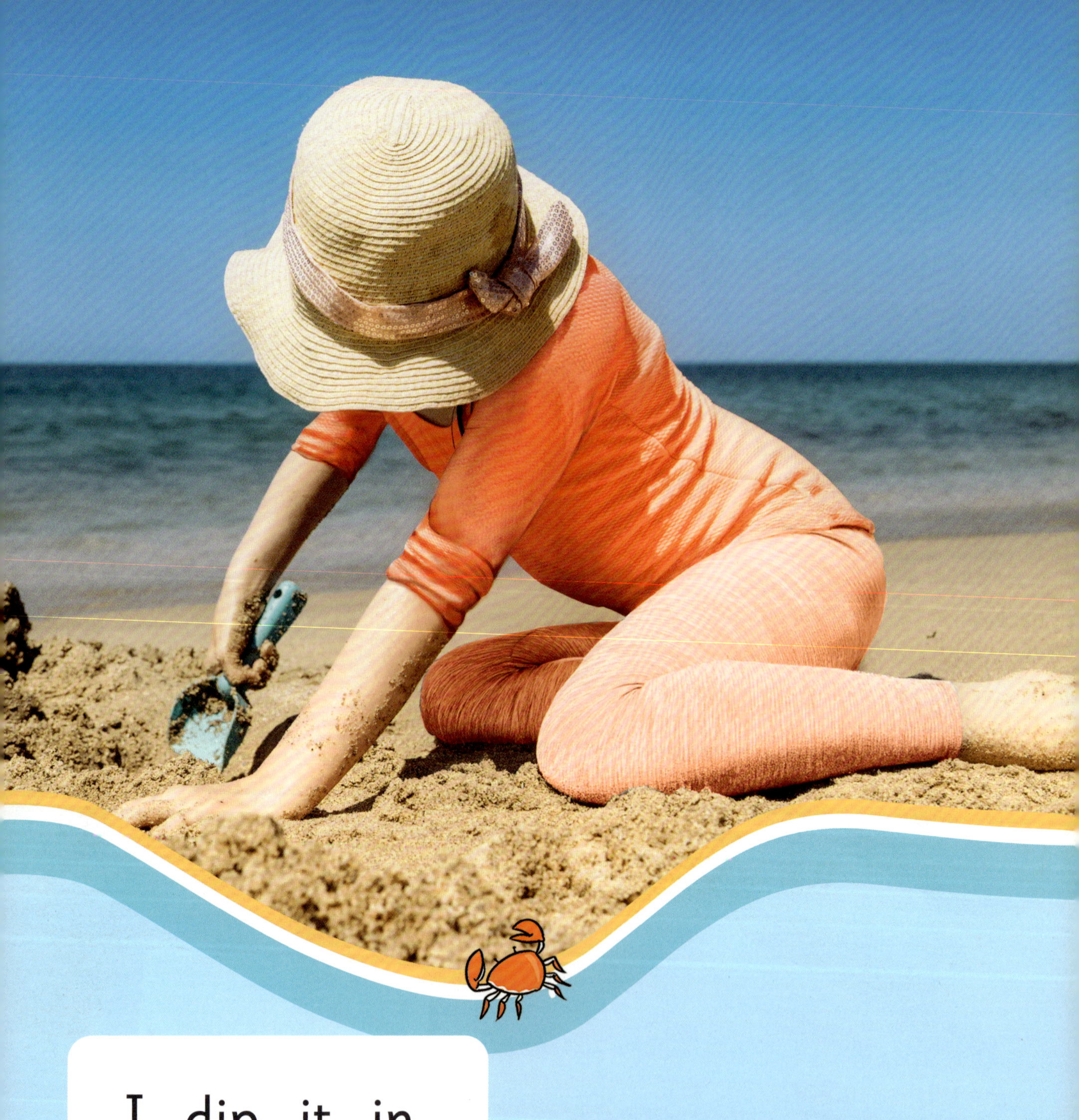

I dip it in.

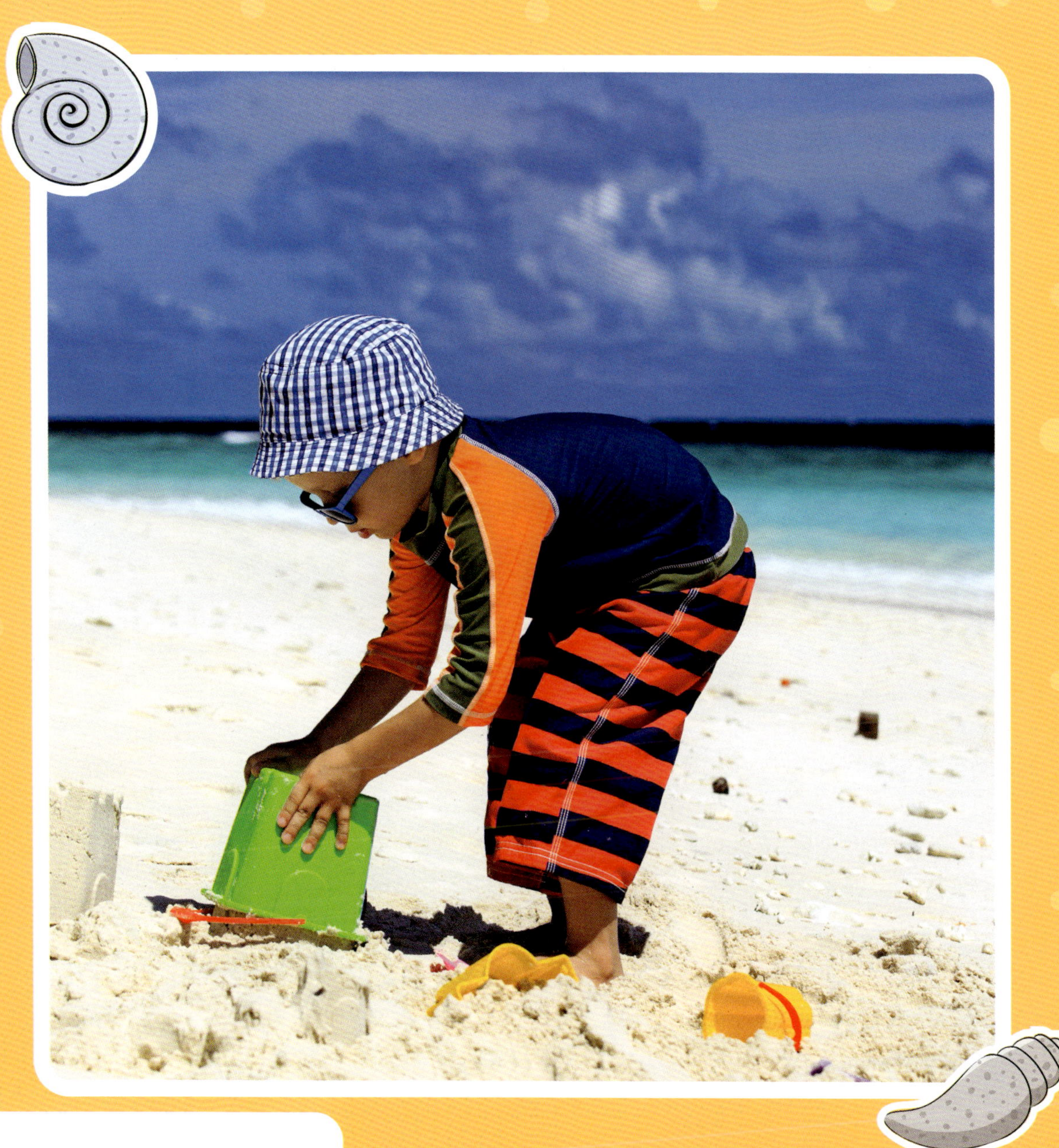

I tip it.

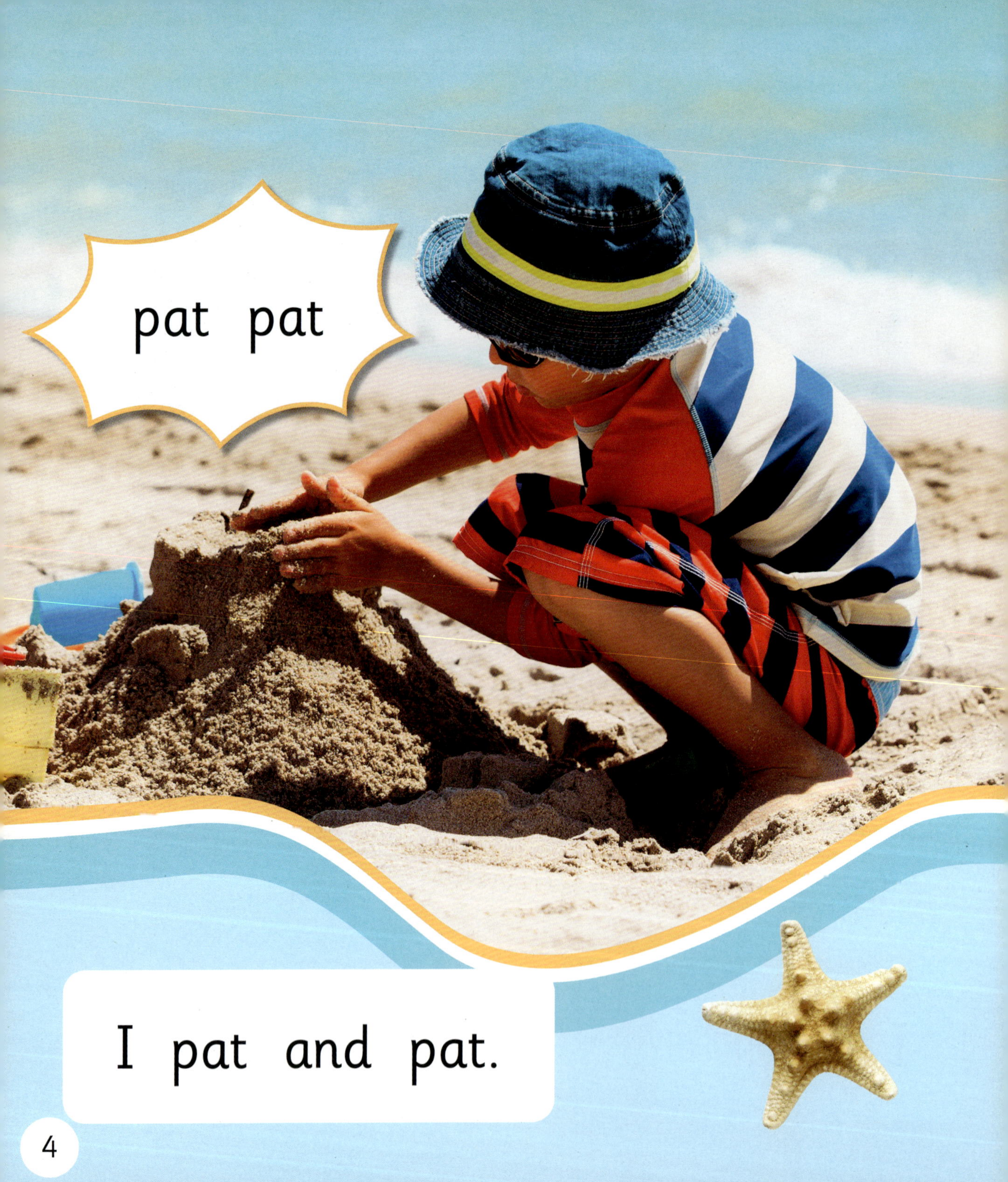

I pat and pat.

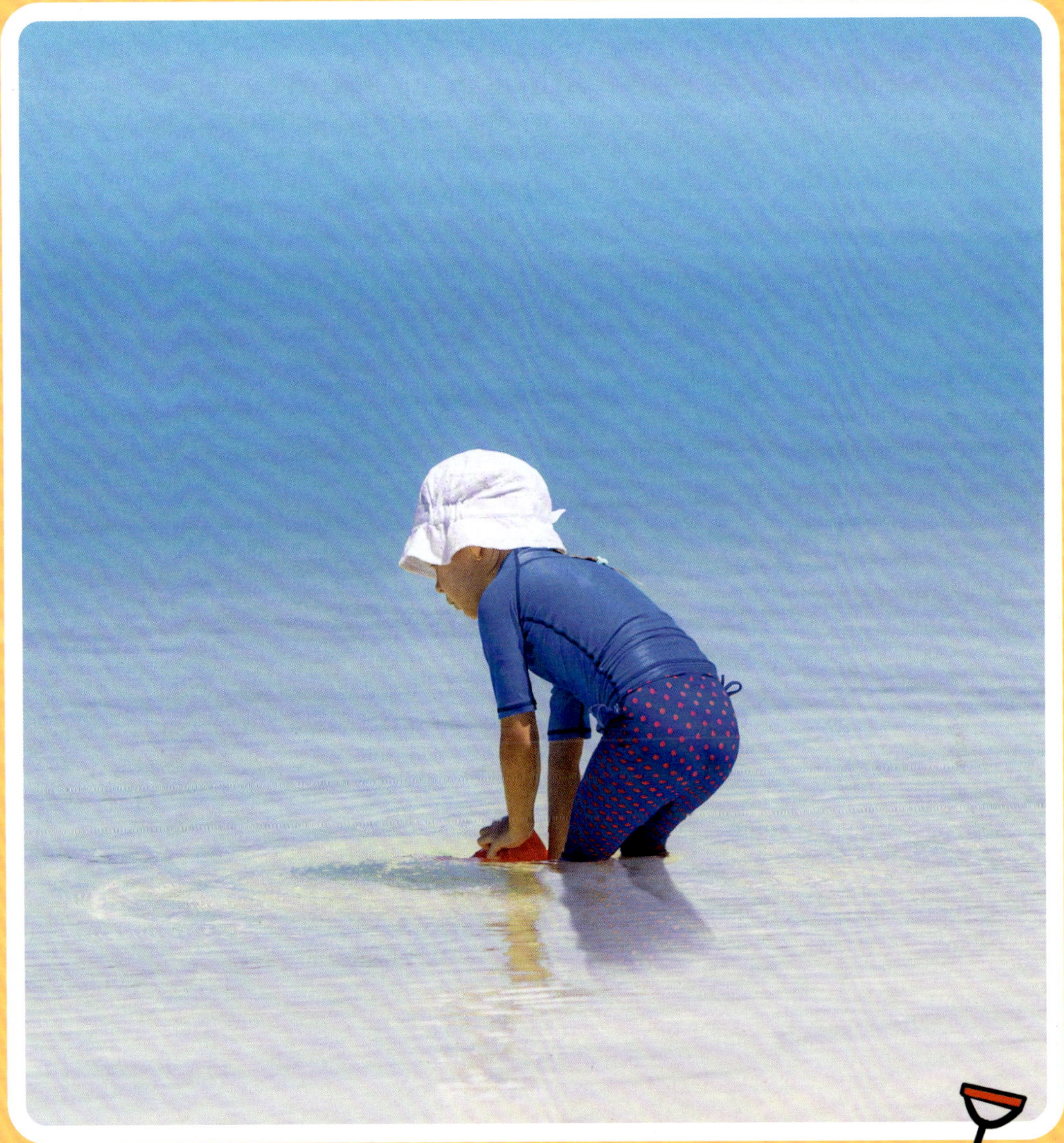

I dip it in.

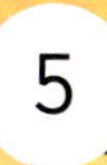

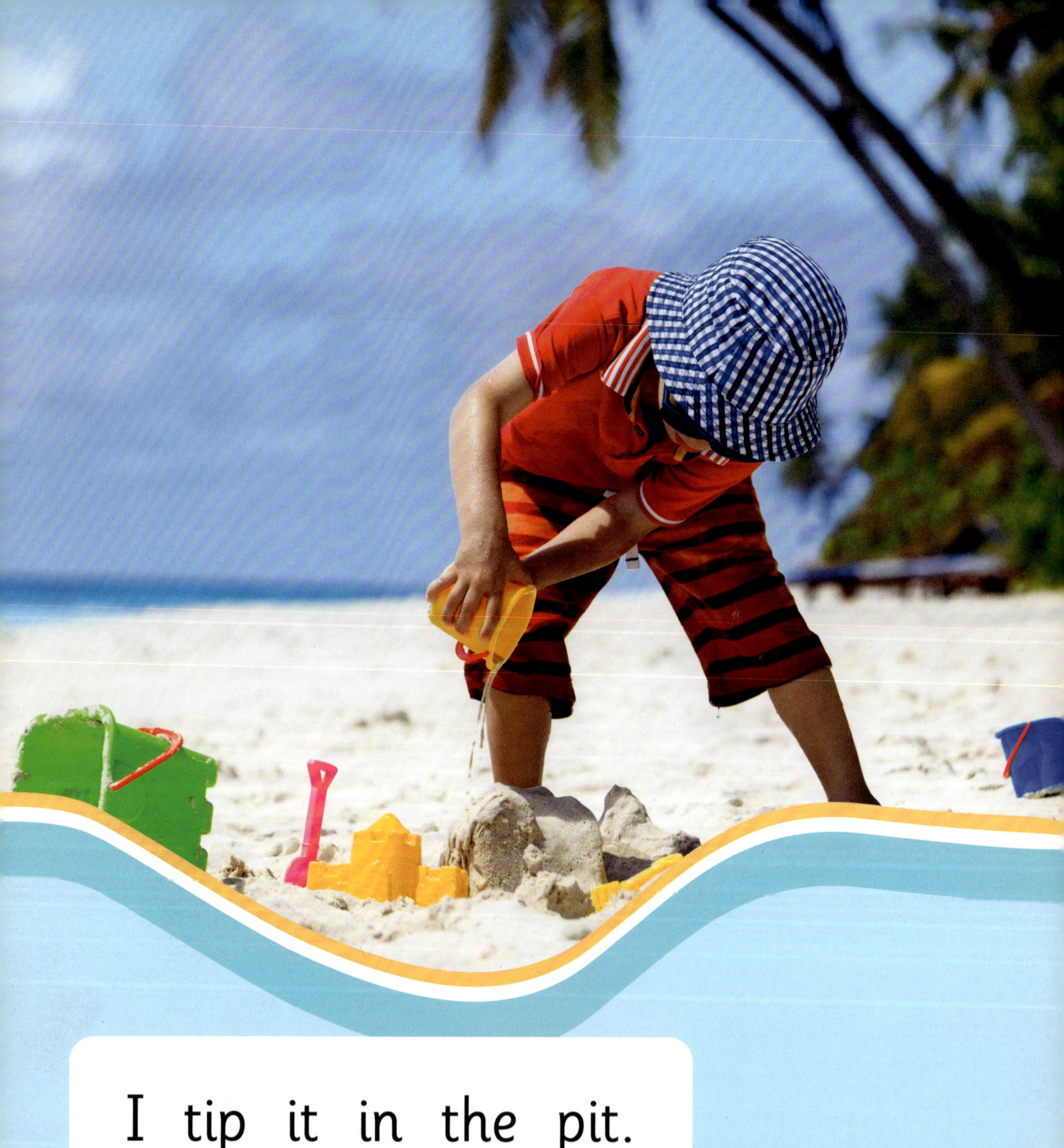

I tip it in the pit.

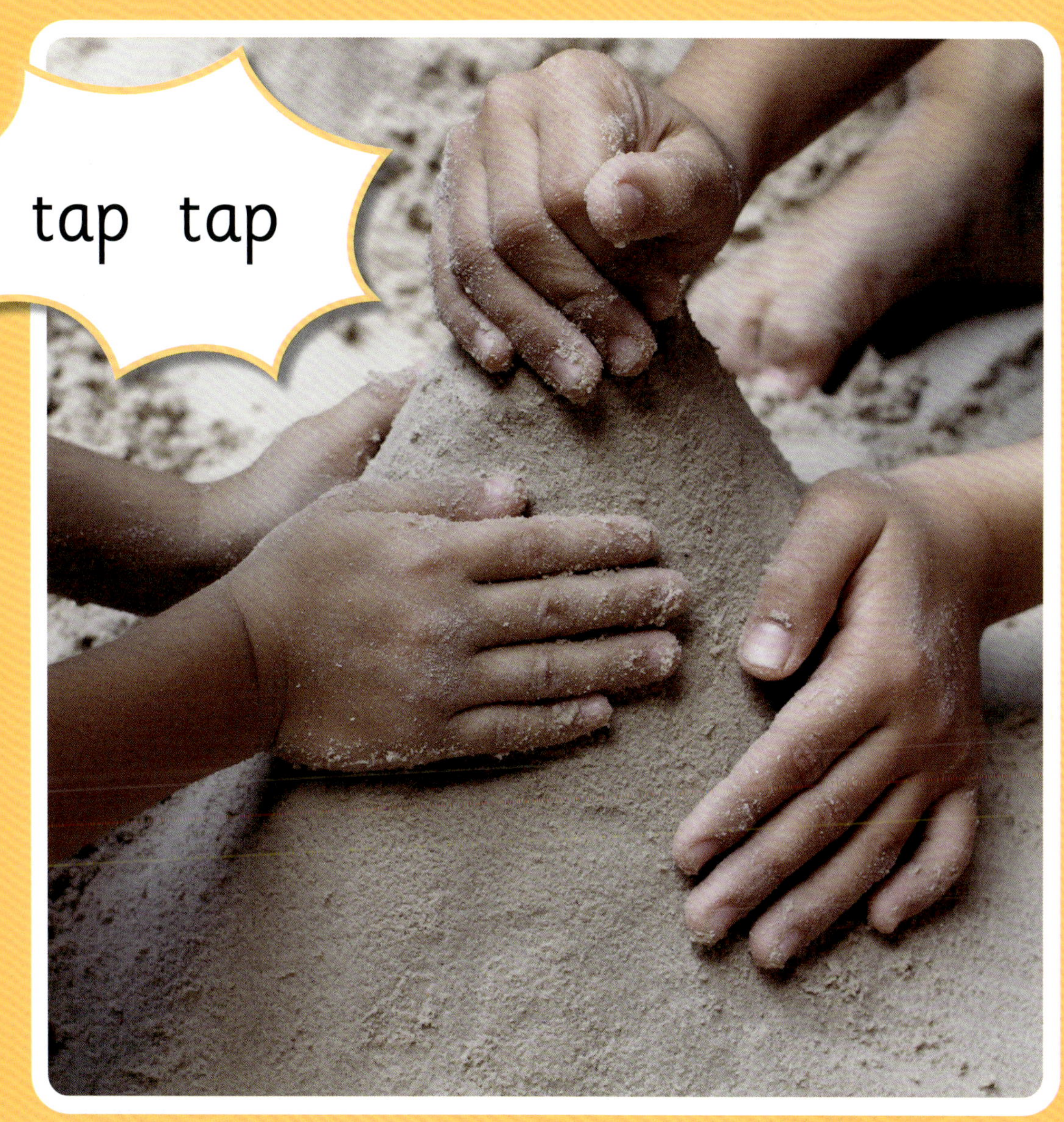

Tim and Min tap it.

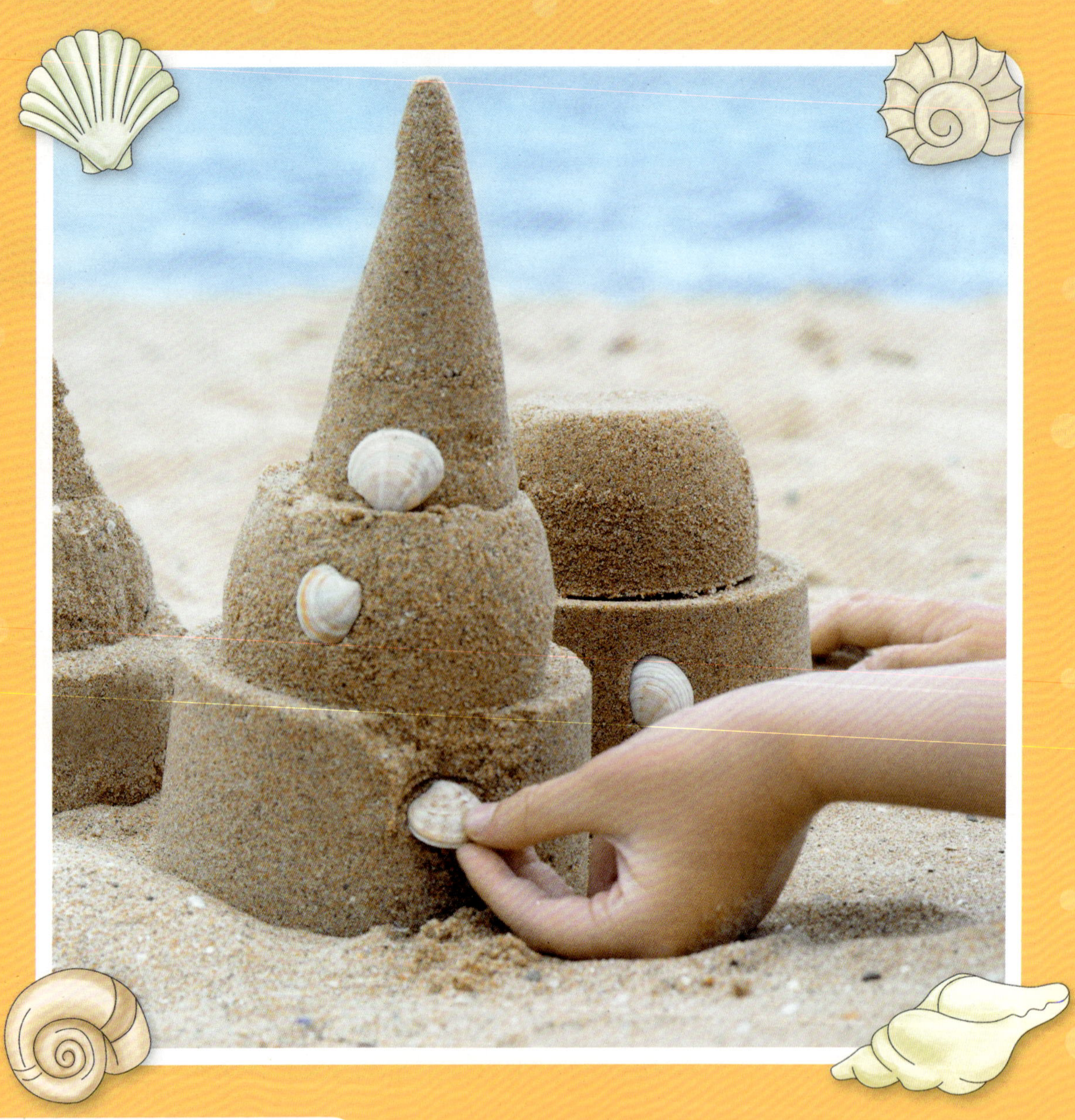

I pin it.

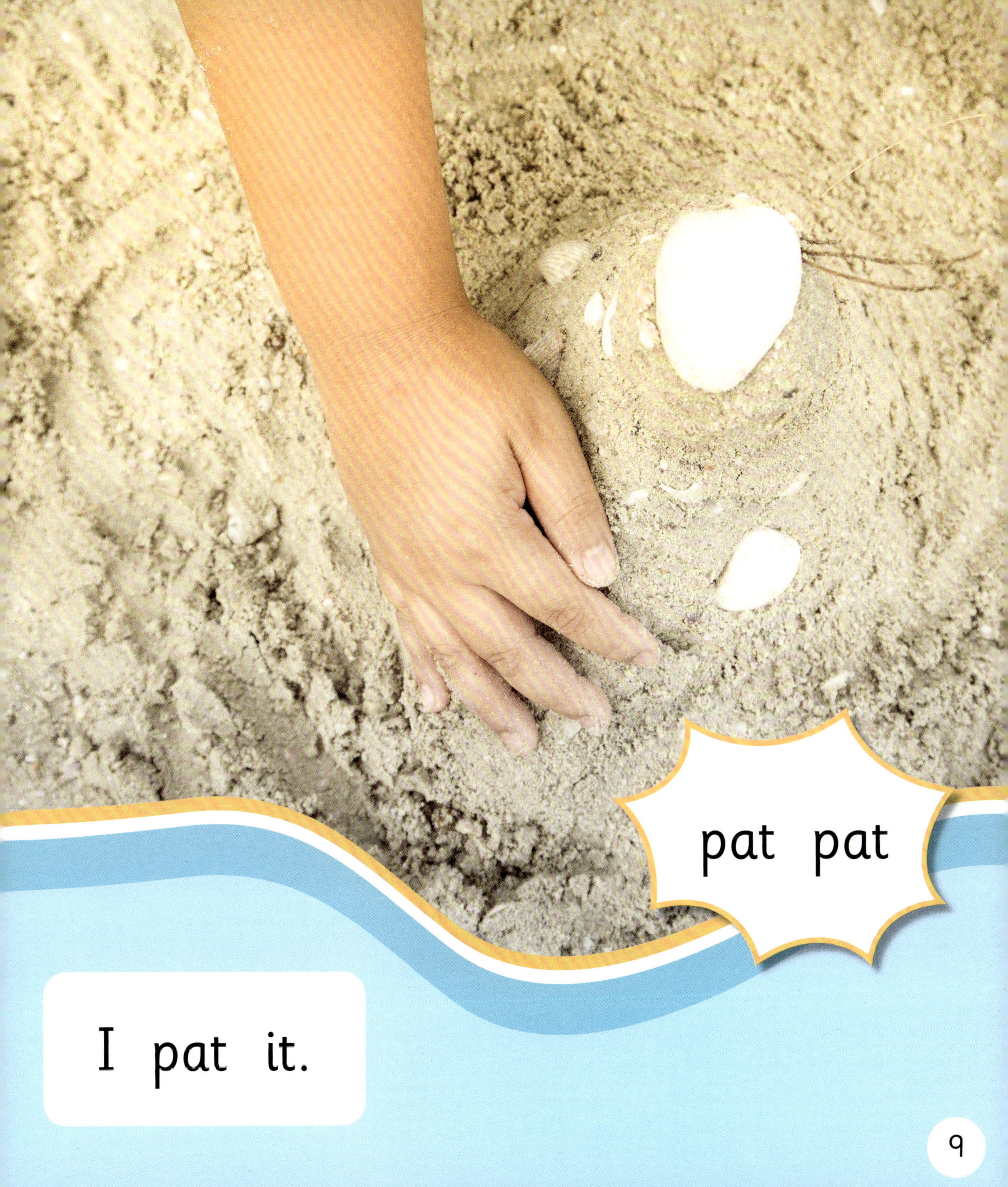

I pat it.

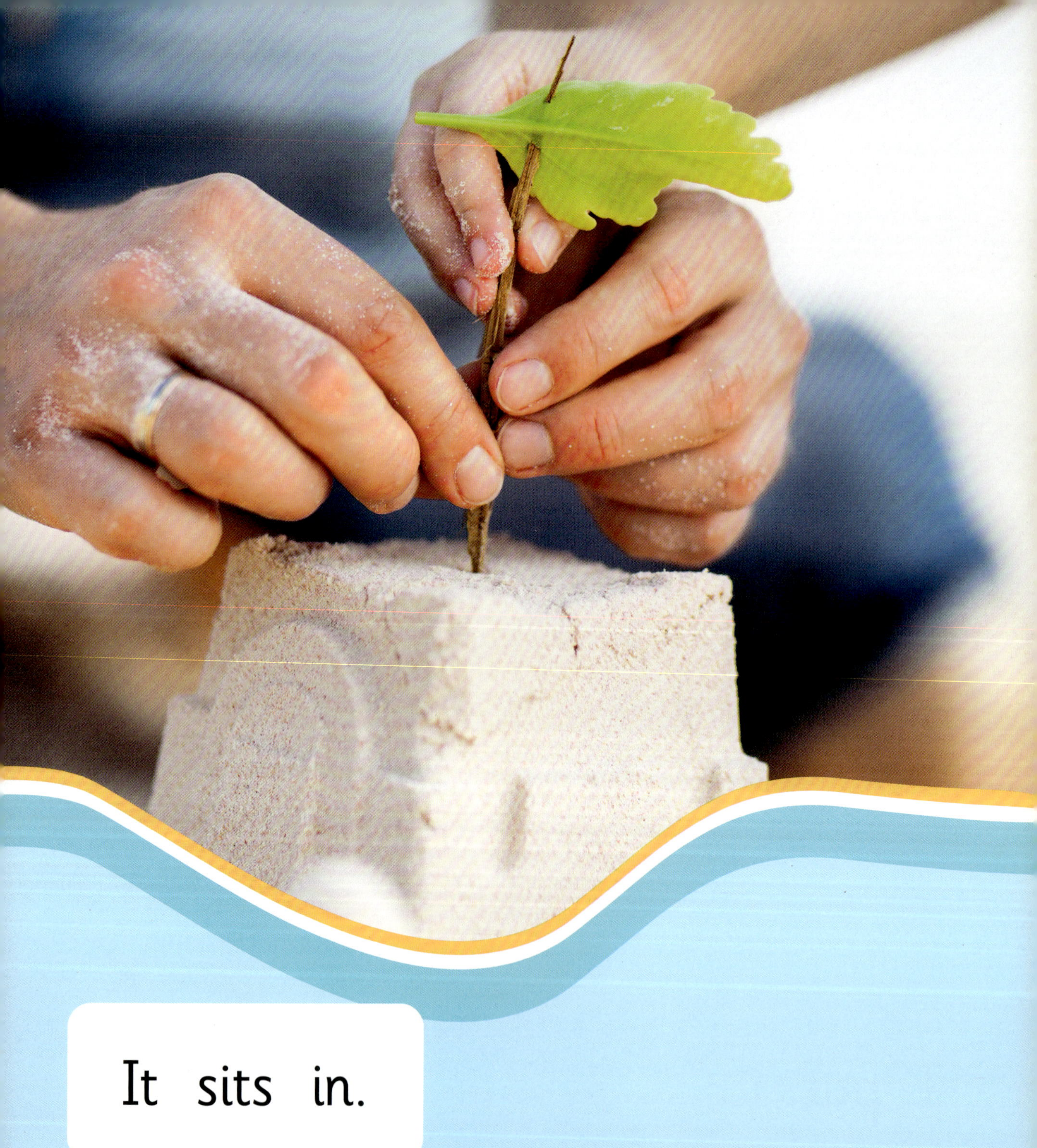

It sits in.

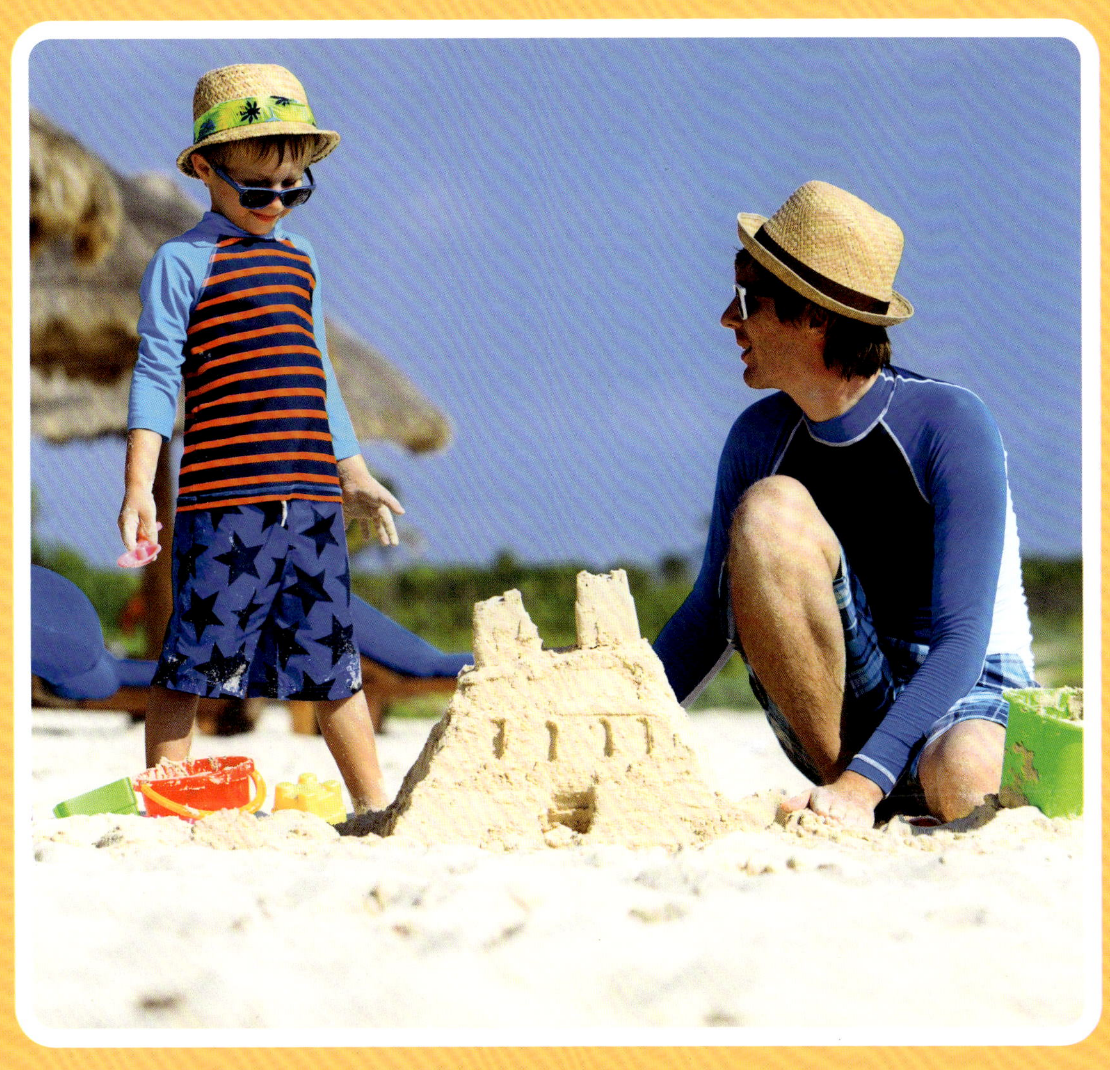

Dad and I did it!

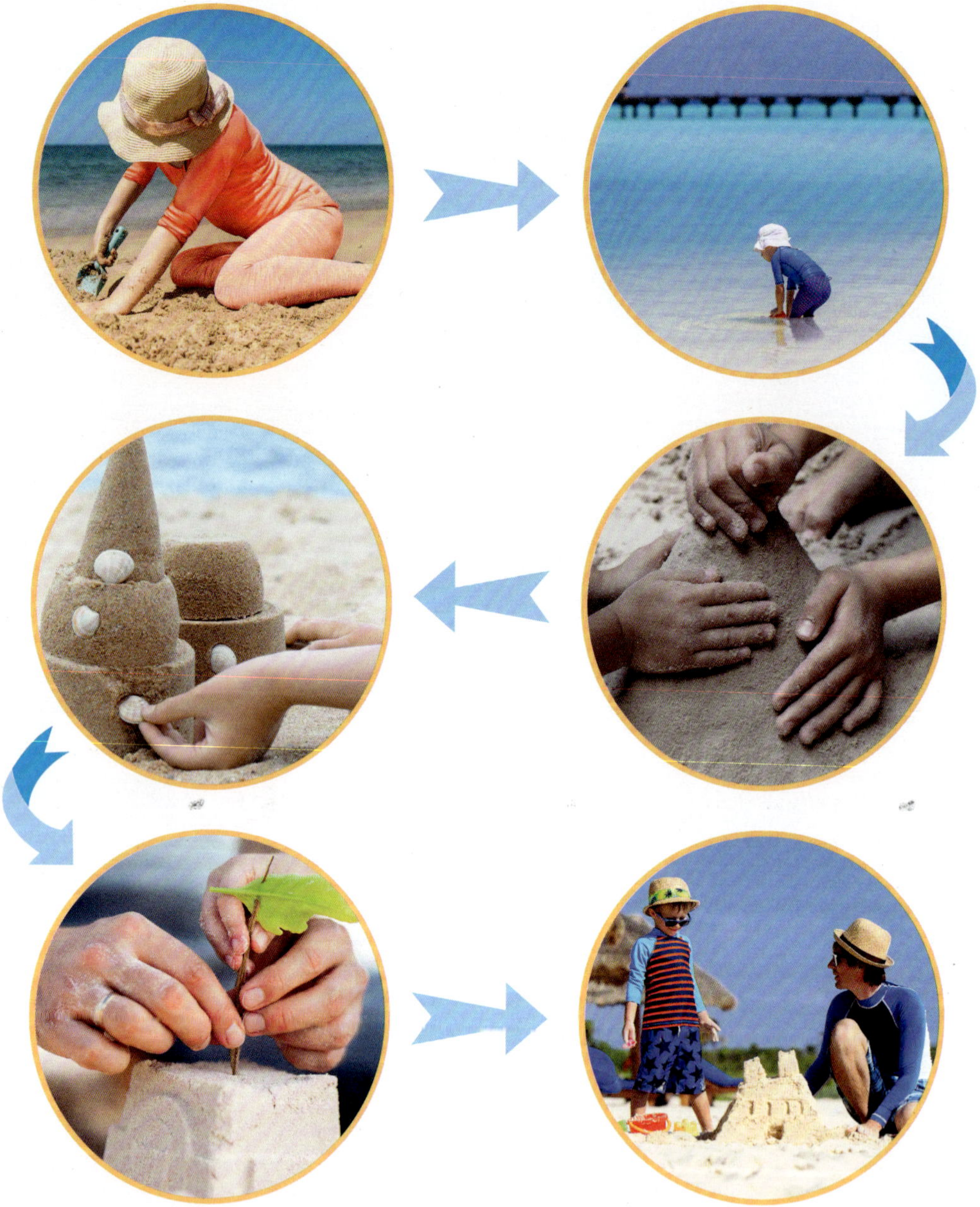

Encourage students to use the images to retell the story.